EDGE BOOKS

Robots

AWESOME SPACE Robots

BY MICHAEL O'HEARN

CONSULTANT:
REID SIMMONS, PHD
CARNEGIE MELLON UNIVERSITY, ROBOTICS INSTITUTE
PITTSBURGH, PENNSYLVANIA

CAPSTONE PRESS
a capstone imprint

Edge Books are published by Capstone Press,
1710 Roe Crest Drive, North Mankato, Minnesota 56003
www.capstonepub.com

Library of Congress Cataloging-in-Publication Data
O'Hearn, Michael, 1972–
Awesome space robots / by Michael O'Hearn.
p. cm.—(Edge books. Robots)
Summary: "Describes various robots and robotic probes used to study space and explore extraterrestrial bodies"—Provided by publisher.
Includes bibliographical references and index.
ISBN 978-1-4296-9918-1 (library binding)
ISBN 978-1-62065-778-2 (paperback)
ISBN 978-1-4765-1557-1 (ebook PDF)
1. Space robotics—Juvenile literature. 2. Space probes—Juvenile literature. 3. Outer space—Exploration—History—Juvenile literature. I. Title.
TL1097.O44 2013
629.43'5—dc23 2012033234

Editorial Credits
Aaron Sautter, editor; Ted Williams, designer; Eric Gohl, media researcher; Laura Manthe, production specialist

Photo Credits
Getty Images: National Geographic/Pierre Mion, 5; NASA: 13 (top), 14–15, 17, 20, 25, 28, ESA/M. Livio and the Hubble 20th Anniversary Team (STScl), 13 (bottom), GSFC, 29, JPL-Caltech, cover, 7, 9, 11, 19, 23, 26, 27, JPL-Caltech/Space Science Institute, 6, JPL-Caltech/University of Arizona, 24

Design Elements
Shutterstock

Printed in the United States 5265

Table of CONTENTS

A Giant Leap for Robot-Kind

Astronaut Neil Armstrong was about to make history. On July 16, 1969, the *Apollo 11* lunar module landed gently on the Moon. As Armstrong stepped onto the Moon's surface, he said famously, "That's one small step for man, one giant leap for mankind." However, robots had already landed on the Moon years before.

Crash Landing

The first U.S. space robot to reach the Moon was *Ranger 7* on July 31, 1964. *Ranger 7*'s mission was simple—take photos of the Moon while crashing into its surface.

Over the next few years, the National Aeronautics and Space Administration (NASA) sent several more robotic explorers to study the Moon. Each one helped scientists learn more about the Moon and how to travel safely in space. Today several high-tech space robots play a key role in exploring space and our **solar system**.

solar system—the Sun and the planets, moons, and other objects that move around it

Ranger 7 sent more than 4,000 high-quality images to Earth before crashing into the Moon.

ROBOT FACT

In the 1950s and 1960s, the Soviet Union sent several robots to explore space and the Moon including *Sputnik* and *Luna 9*. The Soviets' *Lunokhod 1* was the first successful rover to explore another world.

Types of Space Robots

Like all robots, every space robot has certain necessary parts. Space robots are equipped with sensors and computers to see and respond to their surroundings. They also carry the tools and power sources needed to do their jobs.

There are four main types of space robots—probes, orbiters, landers, and rovers. Each is designed to perform different tasks. Probes are usually sent on simple missions. They fly past planets, moons, comets and **asteroids** to take photos and scientific measurements.

Orbiters like *Cassini* help scientists study a planet's moons, rings, and atmosphere.

Scientists use rovers to explore and examine a planet's surface.

Orbiters are similar to probes, but they stay in orbit over a planet or moon for a long time. These robotic explorers help scientists study changes in a planet's weather or surface over time.

Landers and rovers are both used to get an up-close look at the surface of a planet or moon. Landers park in one spot and study a small part of a planet's surface. Rovers are the most active of all space robots. They're designed to drive around and explore a wide area.

asteroid—a large space rock that moves around the Sun

Building a Robotic Explorer

Most space robots don't look like robots from *Star Wars* or other movies. Space robots tend to be awkward-looking machines. They are built to carry the sensors, tools, and power sources needed to complete their missions.

Built for Answers

Before building a space robot, scientists decide on questions they want answered. Then they figure out how to build a robot explorer that can get the information they want. For example, to learn if a planet once had water, scientists might need to study rocks beneath the planet's surface. A robot would need to have drilling, grinding, and scooping tools to collect rock samples. It would also need instruments to study the samples. Scientists then design the robot to safely land on the planet's surface and use the tools effectively.

Scientists test every part of a space robot to make sure it will be able to complete its mission.

Built to Last

Before sending robots into space, they are carefully tested. Scientists often build extra robot models for testing purposes. Special machines shake them violently to see if they can survive a launch or landing. Robots are also exposed to extreme heat and cold to imitate the harsh conditions of space.

Big Computer Brains

Space robots are equipped with computers to carry out their missions. Scientists use radio signals to send instructions to robots. However, the great distance between Earth and a robot's location makes it impossible to control in real time. The robots' computers and programming help them navigate, manage data, and respond to **malfunctions** on their own.

No Outlets in Space

Space robots would be useless without a source of power. Most rely on solar power and rechargeable batteries during their long journeys. The large "wings" on many space probes are made of solar cells. They gather the Sun's energy and turn it into electricity, which keeps the batteries charged. Space robots often rely on **nuclear power** as well. Nuclear energy provides power for missions that last for many years.

malfunction—failure to work correctly

nuclear power—power created by splitting atoms; atoms are the smallest part of a substance

Dangerous Dust

Dust is a dangerous enemy for high-tech space robots. Robotic explorers carry many sensitive tools. Dust can ruin the quality of the information collected by these tools. While building the robots, engineers work in dust-free rooms. They also wear protective clothing to keep hair and dead skin cells away from the sensitive equipment.

Robots Over Earth

NASA has sent many robotic explorers to learn about our solar system. However, some of the most useful space robots can be found just above Earth.

The Hubble Telescope

The best telescopes on Earth are huge devices measuring many feet across. But Earth's atmosphere distorts the light that comes from stars. In spite of their size, big telescopes are unable to get a clear picture. The Hubble Space Telescope avoids this problem by orbiting above the Earth's atmosphere. Named after astronomer Edwin Hubble, this robotic space explorer has helped scientists learn a great deal about the universe.

ROBOT FACT

Using measurements taken by the Hubble Space Telescope, scientists estimated the universe to be about 14 billion years old.

"Mystic Mountain" nebula

The Hubble Space Telescope was launched in 1990. It has taken thousands of amazing pictures of stars, galaxies, and glowing dust clouds called nebulas.

Robotic Arms

Large robotic arms are used to do a lot of heavy lifting in space. The Canadarm was a big success on NASA's space shuttles. It was used for lifting and moving heavy equipment in the shuttles' cargo bays.

Canadarm2

Astronauts have been living and working on the *International Space Station* (*ISS*) since 2000. The *ISS* is equipped with the stronger and more advanced Canadarm2. It can lift more than 250,000 pounds (113,000 kilograms) of equipment. Its hand unit can also gently grab and move objects. Astronauts often use the robotic arm for station maintenance.

Robonaut 2

Robonaut 2 (R2) was delivered to the *ISS* in 2011. R2 sees through several cameras hidden behind its face shield. It also has arms and fingers that perform much like those of a human. R2 is currently used for testing airflow in the station's air vents. Scientists want to see if the robot can do other jobs in the future that might be too boring or dangerous for astronauts.

Where No One Has Gone Before

People have long wondered what the planets are like. So far no astronauts have traveled beyond the Moon. But since the 1960s robots have been used to explore the other planets in the solar system.

Thirty-Five Years and Counting

In 1977 NASA launched the most important deep space mission it had ever attempted. For more than 35 years, *Voyager 1* and *Voyager 2* have been traveling across the solar system. Both *Voyagers* visited Jupiter and Saturn. They took photographs of the giant planets, their moons, and their rings as they flew by.

The probes then went their separate ways. *Voyager 1* continued into deep space while *Voyager 2* went on to explore Uranus and Neptune. *Voyager 2* discovered many new moons and rings circling both planets. Both *Voyagers* are still sending valuable information back to Earth.

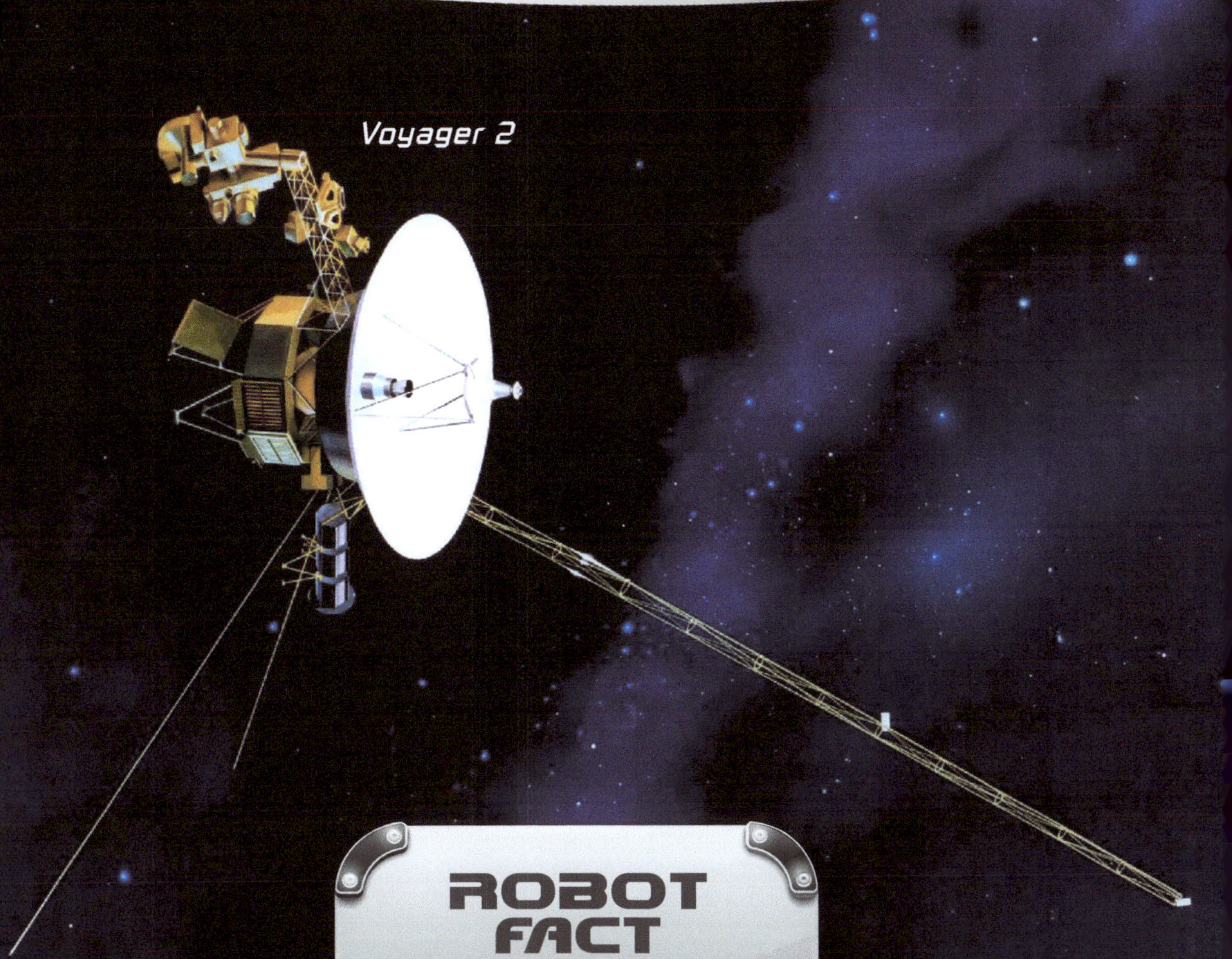

ROBOT FACT

Both *Voyager* space probes carry identical messages for intelligent beings that may discover them. The messages include greetings, music, and scientific information about Earth.

A Robot with Shades

In 2011 *Messenger* passed Mercury twice before settling into orbit. *Messenger* has heat radiators and a sun shade to help protect it from the Sun's intense heat. The robot's mission is to study Mercury's surface and **magnetic field**.

Lava Everywhere

Magellan circled Venus for four years starting in 1990. It used **radar** to see through the planet's thick clouds and mapped 98 percent of the surface. It also discovered that much of the surface is covered by volcanic lava flows.

In 1994 scientists crashed *Magellan* into Venus to take measurements of the planet's heavy atmosphere. The information they gathered will be useful for planning future missions.

magnetic field—the space near a magnetic body in which magnetic forces can be detected

radar—a device that uses radio waves to locate an object or map its surface

ROBOT FACT

Light from the Sun is about 11 times brighter at Mercury than at Earth.

Scientists used information from *Magellan* to create this computer image of the mountain Maat Mons on Venus.

Scientists used *Galileo* to study Jupiter's four major moons: Europa, Ganymede, Callisto, and Io (left).

Studying Jupiter

NASA's *Galileo* explorer began its mission to Jupiter in 1989. It reached the solar system's largest planet in 1995. Part of *Galileo*'s mission was to launch a probe to study the planet's atmosphere. The robotic probe discovered wind gusts of 400 miles (644 kilometers) per hour. It also tracked lightning storms a thousand times larger than any recorded on Earth. In 2003 *Galileo*'s systems began to fail and NASA crashed it into Jupiter's atmosphere.

In 2011 NASA launched *Juno,* which will reach Jupiter in 2016. Scientists plan to use *Juno* to study Jupiter's atmosphere and magnetic field. They hope that learning about Jupiter will help them learn more about how the solar system was formed.

A Far Out Landing

In 1997 NASA launched the *Cassini* orbiter, which reached Saturn in 2004. Its mission was to explore Saturn's moons. *Cassini* discovered water ice geysers on Saturn's moon Enceladus. It also found liquid **methane** lakes on Titan, Saturn's largest moon.

In 2005 *Cassini* released the *Huygens* lander to land on Titan. It was the farthest landing any craft has made from Earth so far. After landing, *Huygens* began studying Titan's atmosphere and taking photos of the surface.

methane—colorless, flammable gas; methane becomes a liquid at extremely cold temperatures

Scientists used *Cassini* to learn more about Saturn's moons, rings, and atmosphere.

ROBOT FACT

The robotic explorer *New Horizons* was launched in 2006. It will give scientists their first close-up look at the dwarf planet Pluto in 2015.

Exploring the Red Planet

Mars has long captured people's imaginations. After astronauts landed on the Moon, many people wondered if Mars would be next. Perhaps one day, humans will get to see the red planet in person. But until then, robot explorers are paving the way.

The *Viking* Landers

The first robots to successfully land on Mars were *Viking 1* and *Viking 2* in 1976. The two landers could not move around the planet. However, they were equipped with cameras and robotic "scoop" arms to study soil samples. *Viking 1* operated successfully until 1982, and *Viking 2* ran until 1980. The two landers sent thousands of photos and measurements of Mars' surface back to Earth.

model of a *Viking* lander

The *Pathfinder/Sojourner* mission was the first to use a system of airbags to safely land a robotic explorer on a planet's surface.

Sojourner's Pioneering Mission

On July 4, 1997, the Mars *Pathfinder* lander came to rest on the surface of Mars. Inside the lander was *Sojourner*, the first rover to explore Mars. The small rover never traveled far from the lander. But it collected a great deal of information about Mars' weather, atmosphere, and land. The success of *Pathfinder* and *Sojourner* served as a model for the next rovers to explore Mars.

Spirit and *Opportunity* Arrive

In 2004 the twin rovers *Spirit* and *Opportunity* bounced to a stop on Mars. They arrived at opposite sides of the planet and began exploring the harsh terrain. The rovers' unique cameras and computers allowed them to plan their own paths over the rocky land. They also had robotic arms and grinding tools to study rocks.

The two robotic explorers discovered salts, **minerals**, and other signs that water once existed on Mars. Both rovers explored for years until *Spirit* stopped communicating in 2010. But *Opportunity* continues to slowly and steadily explore the red planet.

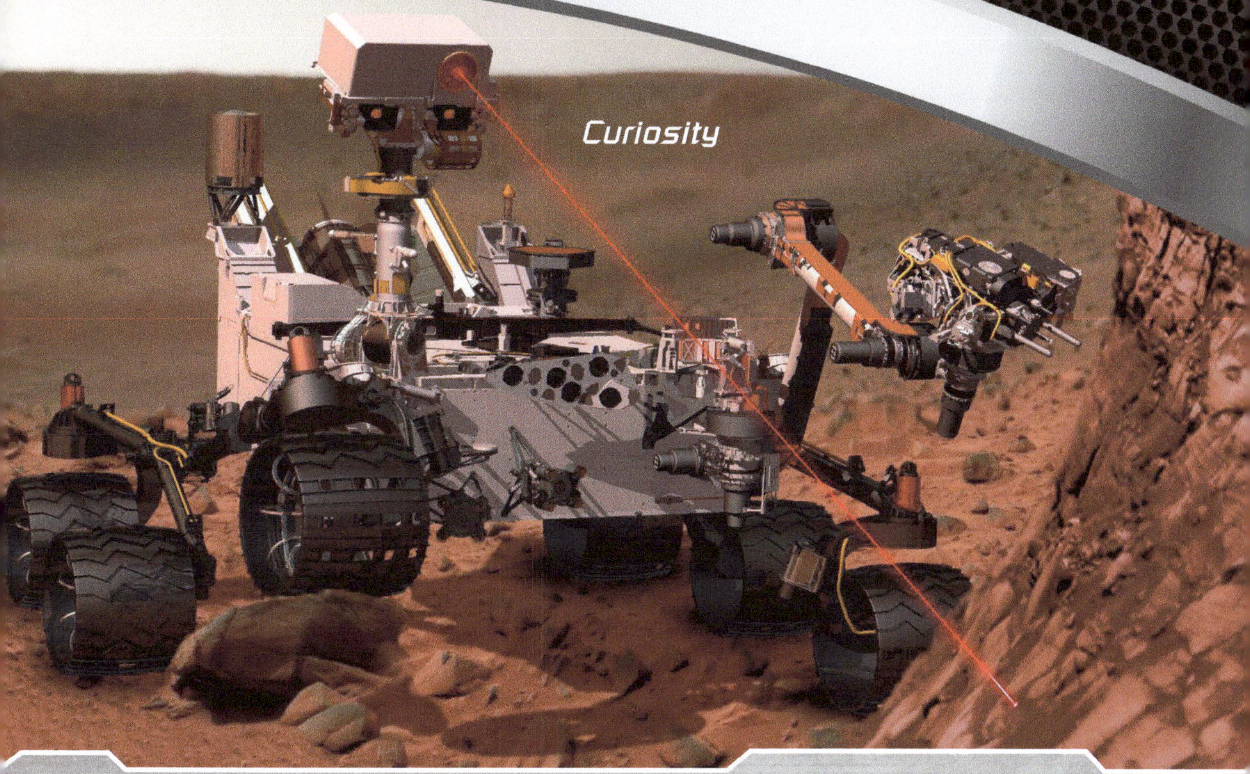

Curiosity

The Curious New Kid

The new *Curiosity* rover landed on Mars in August 2012. Previous Mars rovers were quite small. But *Curiosity* is the size of a car. This roving robotic science lab is equipped with a **laser** to zap rocks and study their makeup. Several other instruments will test soil samples. Scientists hope the samples will help them learn if microscopic life once existed on Mars.

mineral—a substance found in nature that is not made by a plant or animal

laser—a thin, intense, high-energy beam of light

A Bright Future

Scientists continue to plan new missions and build new robotic explorers to achieve them. The Mars Atmosphere and Volatile EvolutioN (*MAVEN*) mission is set to launch in late 2013. Its mission is to study Mars' atmosphere and learn how the planet's climate has changed over time.

ROBOT FACT

In 1983 *Pioneer 10* became the first space robot to travel beyond our solar system. Launched in 1972, *Pioneer 10* continued sending signals to Earth until January 2003.

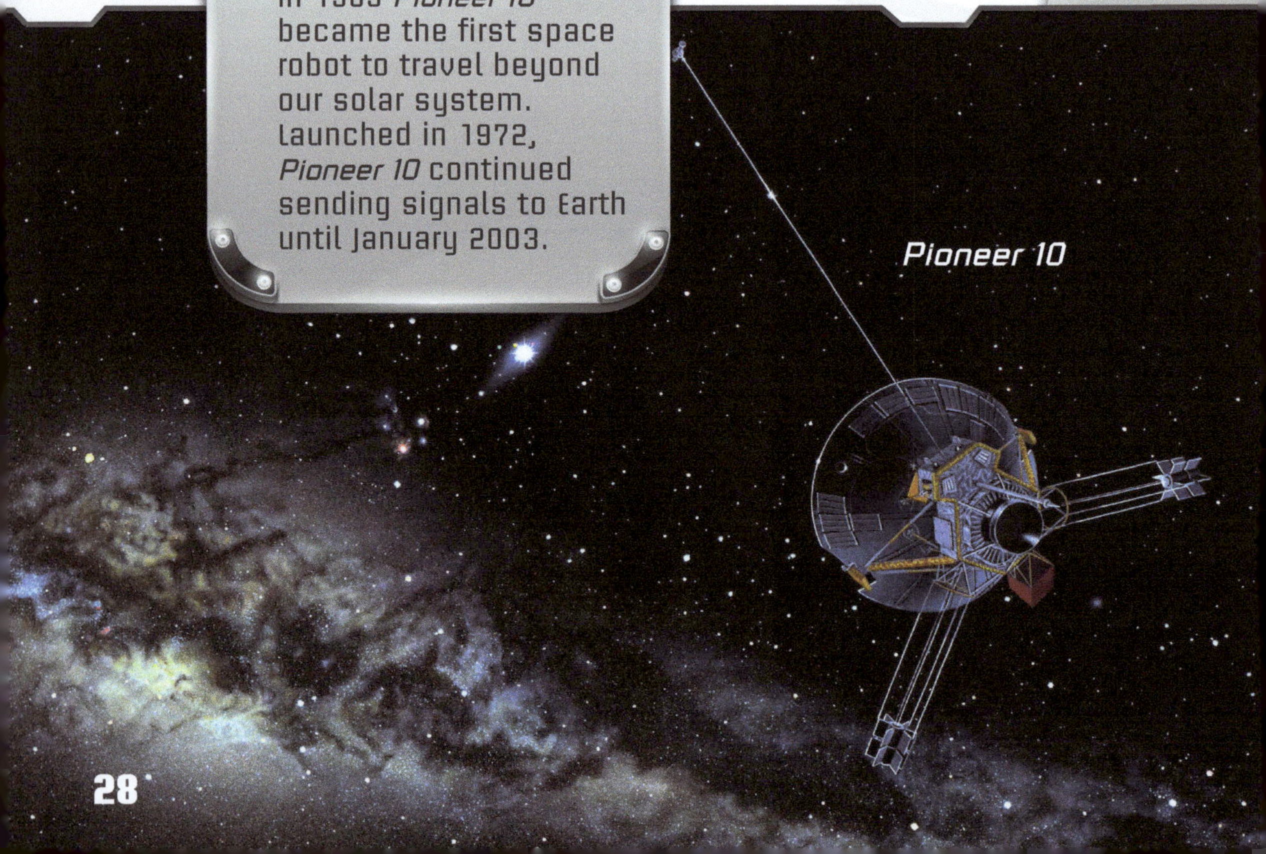

Pioneer 10

Scientists hope that *MAVEN's* discoveries will help them predict the future of Earth's atmosphere.

Space robots have made many fantastic discoveries. They've gathered information about our own solar system and deep space. Robotic space explorers will continue to help us learn more about space for many years to come.

Glossary

asteroid (AS-tuh-royd)—a large space rock that moves around the Sun

atmosphere (AT-muhss-feer)—the layer of gases that surrounds some planets, dwarf planets, and moons

laser (LAY-zur)—a thin, intense, high-energy beam of light

magnetic field (mag-NET-ik FEELD)—the space near a magnetic body in which magnetic forces can be detected

malfunction (mal-FUHNGK-shuhn)—a failure to work correctly

methane (meth-AYN)—colorless, flammable gas; methane becomes a liquid at extremely cold temperatures

mineral (MIN-ur-uhl)—a substance found in nature that is not made by a plant or animal

nuclear power (NOO-klee-ur POW-ur)—power created by splitting atoms; atoms are the smallest part of a substance

radar (RAY-dar)—a device that uses radio waves to locate an object or map its surface

solar system (SOH-lur SISS-tuhm)—the Sun and the planets, moons, and other objects that move around it

Read More

Forest, Christopher. *Robots in Space.* The Solar System and Beyond. Mankato, Minn.: Capstone Press, 2012.

Hamilton, Sue L. *Robots & Rovers.* Xtreme Space. Edina, Minn.: ABDO Pub., 2011.

Kops, Deborah. *Exploring Space Robots.* What's Amazing About Space? Minneapolis: Lerner Publications, 2012.

Internet Sites

FactHound offers a safe, fun way to find Internet sites related to this book. All of the sites on FactHound have been researched by our staff.

Here's all you do:

Visit *www.facthound.com*

Type in this code: 9781429699181

Index

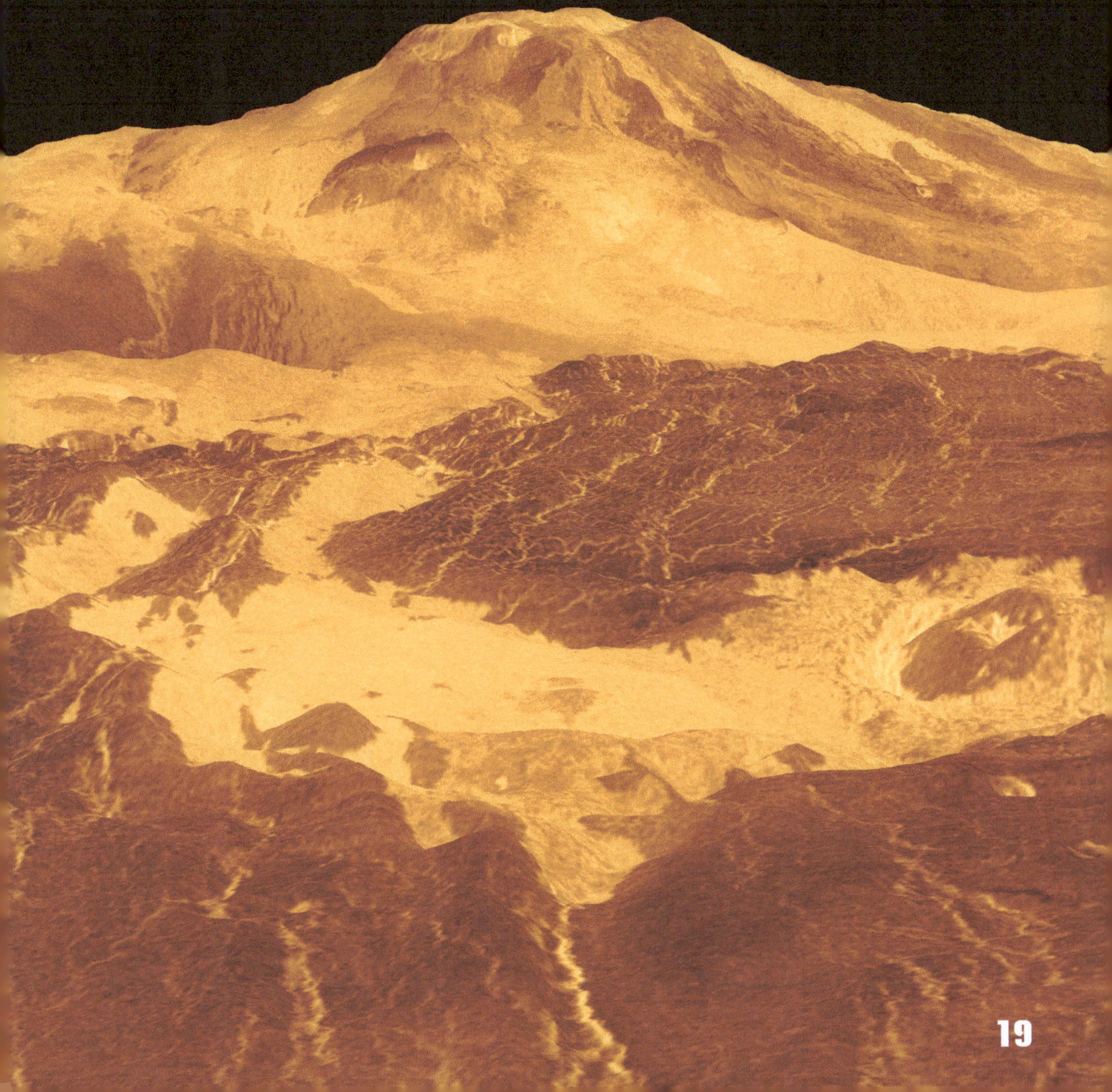

Index